THE DEEPEST P

Anne Elezabeth Pluto

Unlikely Books
www.UnlikelyStories.org
New Orleans, Louisiana

Unlikely Books
www.UnlikelyStories.org
New Orleans, Louisiana

The Deepest Part of Dark

for my daughter

Contents

FOREWORD

who knows how far
the heart can travel
through history
through flesh
through death.

These lines for her great grandmother in the poem "Matryushka" serve as a motif for the larger project poet Anne Elezabeth Pluto undertakes in her full-length collection *The Deepest Part of Dark*.

Here are poems that traverse decades and continents, flesh out the harsh terrain of memory, plumb the depths of loss and grieving, follow the heart's resolve in desire, forgiveness, and letting go.

The Deepest Part of Dark is organized into seven parts, each of which forms a kind of thematic cycle, not necessarily adhering to chronological order, but rather to the underlying trajectory of the poet's voice as it speaks through the poesis of soulcraft.

Part One speaks to the immediate aftermath of the poet's loss of her mother: how that loss rearranges her world, pulls her back into her own childhood and youth, not only in terms of sorting through papers and belongings, but also delving into her own past like an archeologist trying to reconstruct a sense of poetic identity solely from talismans and the physical presence of what remains. To revisit the places and objects of her past in the radical absence now of both her parents is both a challenge to and an affirmation of the power and fragility of memory.

Part Two consists of poems that explore Pluto's Russian Orthodox faith, its iconography and rituals, how its calendar serves as a template for the passing of seasons, and imposes a structure on the mysteries of blood, and faith, and memory: three things that are foundational in all of her work. As is also often the case in Pluto's work, there is an absent "you" being addressed in nearly all these poems, and that absence is what drives the poems both as speech acts and expressions of an earthbound spirituality.

Part Three contains what may be the most startling and transgressive poem of the volume: "Unnatural Acts," a fevered dream of a fantasy in which the poet visits the grave of her Catholic great, great, great, grandfather in Russia and figuratively unearths him from the grave, kisses him on the mouth, breathing life and flesh into the corpse of his body, as her eyes fall on the rosary with which he was buried:

> *a rosary*
> *where I am*
> *the last bead*
> *the end of a long*
> *chain, your marriage*
> *for land, not love*
> *to an Orthodox woman.*

Appearing as it does, nearly at the mid-point of the book, the poem frames all that comes before it and all that follows with a sense of how powerfully Pluto revivifies the dead bones of ancestral history to fashion them into a legacy of personal destiny--a construct of language, myth, and memory:

> *Great, great, great*
> *grandfather alone I pull you -*
> *cold, bones to my coat*
> *kiss your teeth, breathe*
> *air, frost into your suit*
> *it swells, flesh*
> *of the man who made*
> *the man who made*
> *the man who made*

the woman who gave
the child a heart
to see the dead
through dreams.

Part Four begins a cycle of poems about perspective, self-reflection, and aesthetic distance that begins with "Coffee Break in Couplets," in which Pluto looks back on her former self and writing techniques "when I was young with hard dark hair," and compares them with the welcome distractions and obligations that complicate her life as an English professor, wife, mother, pet owner, and compiler of to-do lists that read like poems: "...words that multiply inside my head everything/ sounds like a prayer."

Part Five begins with Pluto shifting to a more expansive line, and a new geographical locus for her language of longing and desire. In her sequence of Texas Love Poems, distance takes on a palpable quality, and the emotional scale of the poems intensifies, running the range from anguished absence to intimacy. In "The Mask" she writes:

I want to kiss
until there is no air
no space, joined together
heart and loins.

I want to wear your face
know your joy, eat your fear
so I will understand
what it means to be a man.

The sequence concludes with the title poem of collection, a poem about a first love who she recently learned had died. As a young man, he sailed away from her, never to return. Never the Penelope to his Odysseus, that thread of her life is seared.

Stylistically, Pluto generally favors Open Form--short, dense, breath-determined but expressive lines featuring strong images and powerful, sometimes incantatory cadences. Her recent work shows some Dickinsonian influence--particularly in its extensive use of em dashes--but there is such self-assuredness in her voice that she is confident in taking risks that would terrify lesser poets. Imagine for a moment that Anna Akhmatova (lines from whose poem "Requiem" serve as an epigraph to Pluto's own "Remembrance Day" in this collection) had somehow decided to flee Stalinist St. Petersburg and miraculously ended up at Black Mountain College in the 1950s with Charles Olson, Robert Creeley, Denise Levertov, et al. That voice would sound much like Pluto's.

In the book's concluding two sections, her mastery of form leads her through a sequence of personal poems that take their inspiration from classical or historical references, or from her decades long immersion in teaching and directing the plays of Shakespeare. In "Portia (After Shakespeare)" she writes:

> *I am such as I stand*
> *and should you want to take me*
> *thus, weighing in the complexties*
> *the ambitions, the sum of me*
> *is the fair sum of motherhood,*
> *of marriage, of vows*
> *of promises I keep*
> *you see me as I am*
> *where I stand, for myself alone*
> *though now for you, to wish myself*
> *much younger, trebled twenty times*
> *more dangerous, more fair...*
>
> *...I am my soul, which is a thousand fair*
> *and burning lights when you walk into the room*
> *where I stand, such as I am*

can you not see me,
the full sum of my love
an unlessoned girl, unschooled, unpracticed
with you.

As befits the rising momentum and cyclical nature of this volume, the poems in its seventh and concluding section take up themes of remembrance and requiem, specifically three strong poems about her father Walter, "Benign Protection," "Summer," and perhaps the collection's signature poem "I have been to Samarqand," which traces his trek through Europe and Asia in World War Two and its immediate aftermath--a sprawling odyssey that had him conscripted into two different armies, deployed on two continents, interned in several prisoner-of -war camps, and witness to an enormous swath of 20th century carnage and migration. The poem, which serves as the coda of this collection, is a tour-de-force that showcases Pluto's lifelong exploration of the themes of language, identity, and the impact of world-historical events on personal lives in her writing, teaching, and scholarship:

I have brought your last book
in prescience and redemption
in secret and in silence
open it, alone, look
study the compassionate
face of Mary
the distant face of Christ
the icons
we cannot escape
imprinted on us since
baptism, I hear you
pray and I pray too
for your life that spanned
the century

The reader is transported across oceans, mountains, regimes and decades, to places that no longer exist, or exist only in the fragility of memory, an echo of the lines in "Benign Protection," where she writes:

> in my reckoning the ghosts of childhood
> remain, incredulous and strong, silent
> and long-suffering, beautiful
> and awful as memory herself.

Still, *The Deepest Part of Dark* remains as much a volume poems of redemption as it does one of poems of remembrance. As Pluto concludes in her poem "Easter":

> ...[the] long lure of love burns
> celestial in the dark
> to domesticate the night,
> each star numerous
> in its power to assail us
> now, in our charter of rebirth…

October, 2019
R.D. Pohl

ONE

THE RIVER STYX

You promised to come back
swore to me that you would
let me know what it is like
the empty landscape – the house
of the father – the river styx
or perhaps paradise. You were
not sure yourself – even in prayer
it was not Christ you longed to see
neither father nor mother – grandparents,
or dead sisters – it was him only
him – my father. I wait for you
each night – I pray you may appear
and tell me the story of how it was
to cross over.

FOG

Dove gray farm weather
inside the house wearing
a sweater – summer solstice
now over – the days no longer
rain in the forecast – horses stamp
in the barn later – led out
to be saddled – my hair in my eyes
fog in the morning – rolls over
by the kitchen window holding
the luminous cups – waiting
for my father – asleep upstairs
beside my mother – the house
the house – its own silent entity
grandfather in the big garden
turning over the earth – grandmother
whispering to the icons – I am
dreaming, standing – parting the
curtains to see the dove gray fog lift
praying for sun – and the world
to roll over.

FUNERAL

When I am dead
be my carpenter
make me the final bed
single, pine manger, lain with straw
covered with fine linen,
alone to sleep without you
wash me yet, while I am warm
turn me supple, wife into child
and dress me plain, in black
no jewels, push back my hair,
tie the bronze cross around my neck
rest on my frozen heart
your hands, hold me there
while I drain perfect
finally into Death,
lay me down
an embroidered pillow at my head
light the wedding candles, let them burn
out the years since first I saw you,
a young man across a room of graves
when in your eyes
the world appeared double
and I became your true wife,
long before they crossed
the crowns above our heads,
and I walked to meet you,
trembling, sit by me, wake for me
do not leave my body,
look at me as you cover
the mirrors and the clocks.

I am a restless woman
even dead
take me to the church
one short prayer will be enough
be priest, confessor
oh husband, lover, my sweetest friend
put your picture into my cold hard hands
and cover my face
piece me to the earth
eternal, alone
in the grave
in the darkness
your face will
be my solace
when last I open my eyes
one final glance
to know
that you were all
that I could miss.

TRUE TIME

The cemetery verdant
in blossom pink and loam
dark we walk – I show you
my favorite dead ground
no one here remembers
us – we watch far from
the tower – a climb close
to hawks and heaven
the dead trees straining
forth to life – my self same
soul attached to yours
no drift of love or imagination
can sever me this purity
with hand held silence
and time spent is time
gained and love made
simple without the body
complications of deceit
and abandonment. I reach
across the dead, the flock
of birds flying overhead
the war memorials and baby
graves – to you – my broken
self – a fixture of a woman
my shame and sin – my secret
sorrow – and pour this out
into your lap – unburdened
stripped down to soul and bone
to render close and tender
this time of life, and sad
season – the return
of spring.

DREAM DEATH THEORY

for my mother

The night world was always open
a series of catacomb mapping where
we could wander in the dark – yours
were populated with your dead – the
beautiful ghost of your aunt who met
you on the high road jumping over the
Cemetery wall in her wedding dress –
without shoes – no one needs them in
the next world where I have seen you
in the apartment across the hall – your
back turned to a stove – a cat curling her tail
at your legs – warming the varicose veins
and leading you into the blinding light.

What My Mother Remembers

A lid to a plastic container
I left in her kitchen at Thanksgiving
a story about a musician who
spent the night in a yama
with a wolf – playing his violin
while the animal howled – how her grandfather
was the only one who wept at the train
station – where she said *Farewell*
to the family she never saw again.

We Russians call the devil to us in every
breath – send someone to him
with the wave of our palms –
and say that only the devil knows
what we ourselves have forgotten.

She remembers being a girl
when Jesus called to her and saved
her from the war from hidden aspect
and torturous hunger – she spent it here
and learned to be
American – the devil doesn't come
to our house – we are too close to
know where he stands or sits or speaks.

We call him to us and push him away
too full of the world to reason with
angels who fell backwards and clipped
their fragile feathered wings.

Yama: deep hole in the ground – used for storage

KITCHEN APT 2E

The smell remains
spice and towels
dust and chicken
ochre walls
and the Blessed Mother
gold and red her son
the flame in her eternal heart
and hearth, til the end
I never remembered to turn
the burners left or right
front or rear, you
want to know
why I took the old refrigerator
with me the glass
cabinets painted
yellow remain red inside
coffee pots scrubbed
to silver brilliance
baking dishes
pie plates
frying pans
and milk
glass salt and pepper
shakers the china
cabinet with turquoise
shelves, an ocean
for your lusterware
teacups and saucers
a drawer stacked neatly
with recipes and outdated prescription
bottles, you saved them

after he died
something to touch
a talisman
to recall
and call
him back
to you.

MOTHER TENDER

Rain brings you back
June and blooming
darkness looming behind
summer ahead sticky green
and hot air
in nostrils you pick me up
each last day of school humidity hanging
after the June shower, polka dotted
umbrella, I let go of once
to see it fly like Mary Poppins
landing on a lawn nearby
Woolworths for notions and summer
books shiny covers for Louisa Mae
the pages unfold like dust, long lost
in faithful timing, notice the rhyming,
the hiding mother tender, stumbling over
reaching, retching, taking cover
me to discover the past like flowers dying
I am alone and simply crying.

MOTHER TENDER (2)

for Gloria Mindock

The bread in the forest
is all eaten by birds – the path
back home will flow without
words – the darkest silence
will be the picture of her – how you
choose without choosing to remember
her best – the laugh you will never stop
to forget – the hopeful place where there
can never be regret – the smell of her books
the chances you took – the final look
backwards – mother tender – what you will
never fail to remember – remains.

EAST 16TH STREET

for my mother

You remain
present always
without malice now
deeply buried you don't
appear in my dreams, as once
you promised. I miss hearing
you speak, hearing you bless
each journey, the worry
in your voice ringing
through me to navigate a precarious
childhood. There is no replacement
for you, no exchange
of heart alike no journey back
home. Last month I travelled
to this beginning
I passed the street
where we had been family
where you lived out your last seven
years where I packed, and sold,
donated and put aside your worldly
possessions. I went to the small supermarket
to find what could bring you
back, what would I buy
for remembrance everything said
your name out loud,
how happy I would have been
to see you, to touch through your
transparency, to have told you
how unspeakable the idea is
that you are truly gone.

Autumn

An hour in the yard – man with a machine
blow the leaves into a carpet of red, brown,
orange, then gold – change blades and
mulch – the bag fills with dust – clouds
of summer dirt kicked up in your wake
the leaves transformed to fall confetti spread as loam
a blanket for the snow to take and hold
the steel gray sky slips behind the houses
on the low road – I know your pain
is unbearable and yet you bear it in the
dust with the dog behind you – I'd rake
them all without your help – my rhythm
established long ago – lonely autumn tasks
stacking wood – raking leaves – arranging
the shed – covering the glass topped
table from the impending storm – predicable
and bold as the unsteady future.

DAYLIGHT SAVINGS

8:00 PM and it feels
like midnight – stone cold
in the half light of
Sunday evening – the cars
pass on making high red
in dark November
remember to turn back,
turn back and gentle
mark the winter's coming.

No Apologies

Night.
Light in the dining room
the parakeet with her head
inside the bell I have made the table
my new desk just to hear her
sing, my possessions surround me
my mother's dead belongings
how much they all had mattered, precious
and presented.

It's already a year after the stroke
her death was everywhere
in King's County CCT sharing a room with
a gunshot victim – his bloodied pads on the floor – soft slippery stones
and two policemen at the door. The boy woke handcuffed
to his bed and she was down the hall – afraid to walk
he took the fall.
The end approached with the inclement weather, the winter
through the cold apartment, her secrets taken apart I found
it all, sealed in my family home, half a century left
to be dismantled.

She never appears in my dreams.
as if she had never been – the green and yellow bird
singing in her small tight world. Sunday evening.
All reflection and no apologies.

RACCOON NIGHT

In October when the witches
come out and sweep their
cinnamon brooms across
the broken pavement
I am breaking boxes
by the light of an almost
full moon under the shed
the scuffling begins
and the beautiful masked
face appears – watching me
on the steps that lead to the deck.
I talk to him as if
he was my dog – watching
his intelligent head cock
to the side – the second mask
appears – a bigger raccoon
listening to my secret dog
language – then a third
Behemoth one squeezes
from under the shed sitting
up almost a character from
Bulgakov if only she had
been a cat – the fourth one
comes – their baby pulled
by sound of my voice
comes close to the railing
those clever little paws holding
the cast iron – my heart
is melting but they know
better and move backwards
a chorus line of masked dancers
taking their final bow.

THIS HOUR WITH WHAT IS DEAD

Your father.
The photo you shared
told the story – you the summer blonde
child in the hammock – shorts,
striped tee shirt, and black socks – nestled
next to your father – in his black jacket –
his worn jeans – holding the book –
How Things Work
Between you – this is how things work:
He was a stranger – the visitor – ready
to jump and run at the sound of the phone
ready to be gone and leave you at home
behind you and out of tender focus lies
the garden – the birdbath and tumbled
pots – the things that could not work
this hour, with what is dead.

Two

CHRISTMAS

I'd gladly follow them
Three men from the east
having watched the moon and stars
forever searching from their Persian tower
where now their tombs stand turquoise
studded blue reaching heaven – did it burn them
into splendor when they packed their gifts
and saddled camels for the journey west
and could He really have still been newborn
or was He already his mother's splendid son
whose uncommon life and violent death had yet to
open - a book we all have read and read again.
This Christmas the story passes through me as if you
had entered - welcome home this star it burns for me
as you – brilliant golden - the light you bring me from the west
your skin as it ignites my own and turned together
into the rope of our surrender - I'd gladly follow you
this Christmas to any manger – where they came too
and brought their gifts – for a healer, a holy man, a king.

Virgin Birth

Born to me
I made you
without the salt milk
pleasure of his flooding
shadow moving
overhead, I made you
without the blood separation
the precious cord
severed in my image
between us
the distance grows shorter.

I am the mother
unmarried
specter you see
near god.
I taught you
from the inside
out of the heart
on the cross
near the star
that shines
from the road
backwards it leads
to the heart
my love
the home
where I kissed
the breath
inside of you
and God
worked the miracle.

Divine Liturgy

One: The Cemetery

The dead sleep
easily, grouped
in threes, they do not
mind us.
it is Christmas
Russian, I am not sad
yet, Nureyev dies in Paris
of a long and cruel illness,
Dizzy Gillespie in New Jersey
from painful cancer,
and we the living
lose our way
to your father's grave
a winter garden of jewish stone
a dark pool, where the skeletons
of trees cast no light.

Your hands
touch his name
three letters, beloved
husband and father I watch
you this silent winter
afternoon, all that silver
blue light cold inside
my dress
I hug my arms to my body
knowing this is your time
to touch the earth alone

your long body
a graceful arc
across his stone.
You are his son
the one of the three
that lived, I am
sorry he never saw you
as a man.
Three geese fly above us
a winter triangle.

Two: Church of the Epiphany

Lost again, this time my mistake,
three tries to find it,
tucked away, a house of god,
Ornate, Russian, onion-domed,
perfumed I did not learn
my religion and lead you
wrong through the icons
Christ and the angels
the rich suffer in hell
but it is Christmas
joyful the faithful move
to the Virgin, to the light
Nureyev is dead
in Paris, Dizzy
Gillespie in New
Jersey, and in Bethlehem,
David's Royal city
someone is watching
for a sign, the star
cast upon your father's stone
the cross I wear, the meeting
of god and the word
and the dance
Gabriel, dizzy
with his trumpet plays
for the faithful
I am surrounded
and the dead

they sleep so easily
on Christmas
while we
alive with our dark hearts
circumspect and wounded
examine the future
accordingly
in the flight of birds.

St. John the Divine

Legend has you
the evangelist, the writer
the one who knew both Christ
and the Word.

It is Epiphany
I am a child
in a red wool dress
the black and gold flowers
move against my legs and arms.
They imprison me.

It is Epiphany
your icon burns
as I kiss your mouth
my heart floats beneath the field
of red and black and gold
You are real
and whisper my name
through the glass and jewels.

THE THREE KINGS

for Vladimir

January rain
water turns to black
ice – no snow
as predicted last year
it was standing room
only
where I watched them pray.
I had wanted to light
your way to Christmas
in the wisdom
the dead possess
you must by now
have forgiven me.
My prayer was to Mary
what I asked for
I received this January
I'll find the candle
and in the church
I'll say your name
among the believers
it will not matter if I
belong this year
I've found a place
in the dark where I struck
a hundred thousand matches
and played with fire.

TWELFTH NIGHT

In the dark the crescent
moon illuminates the road
the river and my retreat.
I'm heavy with stagnation
no room to move
in either direction.
Let Mary take my place
and I will be her icon
assume the silent
knowledge the moment
of birth and joy
the precious baby whose fate
She didn't think of when
turbaned kings laid gold at her feet.
Silent Mary holy Mary
You can have my heart
in exchange for your peace
it's indignant and damaged
but you've seen worse
take it from me
fill its fissures with gold
seal them with myrrh
and frankincense will signify
the holiday.
Wear it as a jewel
and take my place.
I will hold your son
against my empty chest
His heart strong enough
to keep us both alive.

AFTER CHRISTMAS

The tree
sheds like the dog
I planned to take out
by Russian Christmas
but a storm came and
left it naked another week
before getting picked up
dragged away
and dumped
like so many other memories
lost in gold and red paper
in light and ornament only
the candy canes remain
in the cut glass bowl
on the coffee table
the Christmas chocolates
too and Chanukah gelt
that no one touched.
Too much to digest
Too sweet for the taking
and the tree, a Frasier fir
the first tree we all saw
and quickly agreed was
the one sends its needles
falling for weeks I have been
sweeping away
the birth of the savior.

SOMEONE ELSE'S DOG-EARED SCRIPT

Slowly, the daylight lengthens
as the snow remains in sad
patches of items lost after Christmas
and patterns of dogs who ran outside
and came back in suddenly we are all
shoveling shit against the tidings of
this spring where I have lost track
of the daylight - falling asleep over
tests - on planes - driving two and a half
hours to travel seven miles when I could be
halfway home in a different life time was
more important - the winter made us vigilant
no longer surprised by envy - weary of sadness
carrying someone else's dog eared script
in our pockets - it was enough to listen and
nod, politely at first, then shake in the huge
dismay of misunderstood connection - it was
more than enough to hide behind the mammoth
walls of snow and ice - to walk slowly on the shiny
black pavement - we took our lives in our hands
presenting them as gifts - a multitude of magi
lost astronomer kings of the east - each star
beckoned us forward - each coloring book constellation
was the map we threw down before the snows came
before the trains stopped running - dead on long awaited
arrivals and we gave up - retreating to our dimly lit homes
and crackly telephones - anyone who dared to call us
sounded as though they were a trillion light years away.

FLIGHT OF GHOSTS

The incandescent evening
silver snow and hidden moon
opal light on houses imprisoned
by ice dams those stalagmite predators of
winter – you have made us a bold
people – up at dawn to shovel
cars and salt the paths
blow the snow into the air
spun like sugar falling softly
to cover what has already
been made ugly, grey, marked
with mud and tires – prodded
by plows – stomped down
with boots – the piles grow
steadily into battlements –
and rooks the birds
cry piteously overhead
circling wider and then
lost in the incandescent
evening – the final flight of
ghosts.

Two ghosts for the New Year

Easy to resurrect the dead – through
the wire – the elusive Ethernet – the dead
like electricity need energy to come back
Resourceful Odysseus gave his blood
to dead Achilles for conversation -
love to love – man to
another soldier - for me it is much simpler – no
blood given for another girl
who loved you and put your photograph in an album
and for the sake of curiosity I looked never
thinking, nor even in memory that you would appear
there – caught grainy young – no more than 17
turned to face a camera faded now 37 years ago
I can make it feel like yesterday – some pain is so
perfect that it lives forever – a pinprick to stir
the blood I never gave for you either – never cut but
burned – betrayal to transfiguration – I used to
believe I had forgiven you – but given
the chance I cursed you backwards – into silence I have
asked you to forgive me. You for whom this heart
molded as a boy – the exchange of love
so complete that all my decisions
decades later came
from that first break
the distance only
made me want to live. You tried suicide
twice – the ghost of a boy in the photograph –
Happy New Year – the second ghost the man
I didn't marry – now engaged – in the photos
he finally aged – and then aged again

unbound by tradition – a legacy to himself
I can remember and then, and then
forget.

Snow Earth

A cover of snow
to blanket the earth
or just my dreaming still
come to me this winter
your hard warm body
to turn me into beauty
your hands to pull me
through into the new year
let the road lead us
forward stay close
take my hands
two hearts to fall as one
to make this winter white
blanket this snow
steeped earth.

PRAYERS FOR THE DEAD

Hallowed out of the father
are the dead
and on my knees
with shimmering eyes
to catch
their light, brave
pieces of my own
recklessness
orphaned
by war separated
by language
resurrected by myth
each breath
is a prelude
each word I say
is the way back
each tiny photograph
pressed flower
folded ruble
orthodox cross
bottle of spirits
is a reminder
of those unknown
whose blood
runs through me
like water.

RUSSIAN ORTHODOX LENT

Dark period in the wilderness
I walk under bare trees, hungry,
the village wolf
has come to die among
humans, it is an omen.
I walk thirsty, each day
my heart burns down further
by Easter it will be ash
I walk broken, praying my body
will recede, fade away, fall
from my soul and I will be made
over, a small point of light
one tiny star in the Eastern sky,
I walk, eternal, push
icy branches from the trees
call the old wolf back
to me. I cannot bear
to see him
die alone.

CRUCIFIXION

You close the door
and nail it hurt shut
me out of your
monster's heart
small like a newborn
fist walnut sized
and beating
but I am no
where near
the door
have no
hammer
to wretch
it open.
I'll wait
like Mary
the Mother of God
and Mary
the Magdalene
and the other one
whose name I
cannot remember
until
you rise
and walk
from the grave.

DOCUMENTATION

Sigh lanced
like Jesus pierced
I will cry alone instead
of bleed – and plead
what innocence
I ascertain – so tired
of being
my own
advocate. and you
blameless in your
corner – drawing
the line and redrawing
the times I stepped
over it. you need me
to agree – I want to
get out and over,
the rain
as a cover
to wash me clean.

EASTER

the emerald parlor
remembered, come yourself
to convince me now impose
yourself firm to the
maroon furrow
that is my heart.
Interloper, make your mayhem
here, where I have been
miserable - christen me
this burglar
who has stolen time and
time again my sins rise,
duplicate with yours,
a column of white ash,
our own promiscuous rupture
of faith. I will give
you back the way home
assent from the cross
gnaw through me to my bone
and there write beautiful
the names of all
our dead in your salt
milk be my confessor
coax me, plunge sincere
the epistle of silence
handwriting on the wall
and beside me, the cross
lay sown, mount me glaring
move finally bruised
in the disjointed

homily of sex from which
we will abstain, but
not to disappoint, the
long lure of love burns
celestial in the dark
to domesticate the night,
each star numerous
in its power to assail us
now, in our charter of rebirth.

EASTER SUNDAY 2017

There are dead animals in the house
having crawled into a space that will
serve as both cradle and coffin – the sweet
sickly smell of decay coming through plaster
concrete, wood, insulation – no resurrection
this Easter I stop to imagine your terror:
shallow breathing – no space to turn and
retrace the journey in – the journey on
the smell will remain for at least a month
by then you will have become bone
part of the house – piece of the foundation
little ghost paws will make their way through
the walls and see what they can no longer
eat.

BONE TRINITY

They appear washed
up, given from the sea
to the earth, to us
X marks the spot
on the harbor porpoise
its open mouth revealing
teeth, skin turned to black
we have no knives with which
to cut it open and take the bones
as our treasure.

The harbor seal, small
flippers tucked under
its brain still in place
with the spine bleached
it is dead
we are alive
and I ask what else we will
find?

In the distance walking to the path
the third lies
head turned
beak down,
black feathers moving
in the wind.
cormorant.

Time moves slowly among the dead
we stumble over rocks sit behind
the dunes in spring silence

I would stay this way,
nestled against you
small and safe
in this moment
where my breath
comes on its own
I want to extend myself
out over the water,
but can only send small
messages from the confines
of my heart.
Take the dead
tear out their bones
and like Cassandra,
I will read their entrails
to engender our future,
I will make a map of vertebrae
to find my way back
here, where your heavy
heart acknowledges
my longing
where you reach me
through the sound
of your lovely
measured voice
where I see your pain
clearly without
judgment
and mine own
spread still like those three
dead, decaying
around us.

THREE

THE DARKEST DAYS

Silver light
low sun under
December memory
in blood and
bone tender
you slip away
I use dead
objects to reawake
the season where
you held onto
the golden thread
of your century
unraveling into
Penelope's shroud
warp and weft
looming life
and blooming death.

Unnatural Acts

Great, great, great
grandfather
you lie in ice
layers of Russian
winter, in sleep
I travel miles
countries by foot
to reach the night
of your grave
in the Catholic part
of the cemetery
I dig through
snow, ice, break
my nails to scratch
open the pine box
cracked wooden
ornament of time
its silence startles even
me, and you are there
precious bone wool suit
dried red flowers
mark the space that was
your heart - pearls fused
to gems, a rosary
where I am
the last bead
the end of a long
chain, your marriage
for land, not love
to an Orthodox woman.

Great, great, great
grandfather alone I pull you –
cold, bones to my coat
kiss your teeth, breathe
air, frost into your suit
it swells, flesh
of the man who made
the man who made
the man who made
the woman who gave
the child a heart
to see the dead
through dreams.

Ritual

Bedtime
I climb the stairs
incessantly, too
many times
with armloads
of laundry the dog
tripping at my heels
he knows it is bedtime
soon - to bed
down another toy
in his shark mouth triangle
to tug - take me back
to collect - water
swallow the vitamins - check
the coffeepot - washed
for tomorrow
my daughter to tuck in
my husband glued
to football - if it's Monday
night or any other
in between
take off the eye make-up
wash my face - yes reach to
tug the toy
pat the head
undress to clothe
again to bed - too late - to sleep
perchance to dream
too dream too
late to dream.

BRIGHTON BEACH WAS NEVER VENICE

for Lisa Levine

Green water – South pacific
or Adriatic – dream water
Grand Canal to Carnival.
the masks they wore were
not *Made in Italy* intermittent
Mother tender water masks
where they could not go – Brighton Beach
it beckons still – water wave
crashing save, still from the rocky
reef refuge – the teeming shoreline
left behind – an ocean supported
surrendered between two world
wars and a generation, lost
they swam with the fishes, watched
the man in white, who sold knishes
and fed us from their wedding
dishes – sea salty air and shoulders
bare – Brighton Beach
was never Venice.

DEATH TRAP FOR MERMAIDS

I find the fish
hook in the rug
stuck through and
shiny sharp a death
trap for mermaids I
work my fingers and
then resort to scissors
to cut them free.

I find the fish hook
line and sinker in
the rug muck of
the stream shiny death
for the sharp mermaid
scissors - she uses them
to set them free.

I find the mermaid fish hook
fancy tail stuck through
the line - the shiny stream of
a free death at sea.

BACK STROKE

I used to float
at the sound of your name
across the trolley tracks
and through the throngs of students
at the river - I used to float
through the crowds on the subway
platform – every face in the crowd
was your face – every dark jacket might
have been yours – every lie you told me
was unknown then – you were so fine
at storytelling – good at abbreviated confession
good at picking out red wine – good at ordering
good food – good at making sure I knew the price
I used to float at the sound of your name – the
price of your shame – and even in death
It remains the same.

MILK MOON

for Mark Statman

The moon is made of milk
a perfect round sphere, a ball
of spun silk stars trailing over
your favorite Brooklyn saloon the tar
roof beaches where skylights mark
the night like diamonds made of pointed
steel and isinglass - the anchored
ladder - the hanging mop - the chores
that spin us round like tops - the farewell
letters - the last look back - the sun
is rising on your folded maps - the
closing door - the brownstone stoop
the coming winter where you will
be no longer in the loop - the dark street
beckons towards the waiting train - the
light is fading - the waning moon
is made of milk
The perfect round sphere - a ball
of spun silk.

WHAT ENDS UP MEANING NOTHING

What ends up meaning
nothing - a missed train
a lost friend - traffic over
the bridge - through the
woods - a misplaced key
running out of milk - waking
up late - missing the friend
on the late train traffic moving
through milk - a bridge of nothing
across the traffic of the milky
way it ends.

KING'S CHAPEL BURYING GROUND

The dead are pressed together
In the charnel house, an abundance
of ossuary riches, forgotten for centuries
turned to ditches, the crypts are sealed
off, each portal no longer has a door
but grass recedes to form a floor
in the cold spring evening, the electric hum
of skyscrapers distinguish us from the dead.

GREEN MAY

Copps Hill Burying Ground
10,00 thick bone stacked upon bone
to build the city – British
lobstermen in ghost light
used the hill as a battery – cannon
fodder to the Charlestown shore where
I had never walked before
my periphery stopped at the skating
rink the oval circle on Commercial Street
a dollar entrance fee to find
the rhythm of eternal life skating eights in
imperfect time – this motion of forever
a path – a curve – a smooth surface cut
a pattern high above me on Copps Hill
the sun sets over the battery – the light
coming out from the lovely haunted homes – each
built with stolen slatestone foundations
the silence in locked spaces – green
May places –never look back – or fall
forward – the city is magnificently alive below.

FOUR

COFFEE BREAK IN COUPLETS

I never finish what I begin in haste, picking
my way through the rooms, finding papers

envelopes with dates, I enjoy cutting them into
shreds and patches, and filling the weekly recycle

bag to brimming confetti, the dog always brings
a toy in his triangle mouth, and the chase is on while

the water boils in the stainless-steel IKEA kettle a train
whistle, the end of the period, saved by the bell the dog

settles for a cookie and I am drawn away from the confetti
to make a list – words that multiply inside my head everything

sounds like a prayer, the poem I was composing in my dreams
when I was young with hard dark hair – when I couldn't imagine

that time would be presented in envelopes, in pulling ropes, in
coffee breaks and a list that runs me out to the end of the line.

SHAKMATI

I don't want to remember, but I
feel the incidents move through
me like water – muddy, murky, silt
on the bottom – bodies locked
in death embraces – we were stupid
I take that back where it belongs, the
heart cannot be commanded, at times
artfully restrained, but not told how
and what and where to move, there
are moments, when the present pain,
the despair of trial and error evades
me – what I have shaped, with my hands
and time, what I have reinvested in
removes itself by circumstance, then I
go backwards and wish I had not
moved at all.

Shakmati is Chess in Russian

MISHA NA SEVERA

Misha in the north
on the ice – the golden cock
and little bears climb
the trees for the forest
characters to write out
this valentine in sweet
nothing and the full compass
of your voice encompassed
in the room of my heart imagine
the fierce white bear
the golden cock
the little browns ones climbing
as they do in the tales I
read at night when I
am not entwined
to you a serpent pink – silver –
green I watch you sleep - listen
to your heart hold
as the storm rages outside
and Misha joyful in the snow
blanketed earth moves west to
meet us – where we lie together
my hand slipped into yours
calm in the sleepy aftermath
of *kiss you goodnight*
imagine the baby bears
snuggled tight to their mother
to sleep the winter into greening
while Misha rules the white earth

and the golden cock sings
to wake us up
too late, too late
too late.

"Misha na Severa/The Golden Cock/The Little Bears"
are names of Russian chocolates

Matryushka

for Great Grandmother Szarabajka

So many lost last year
and dying still
your life returns
without interest.
My heart is not a trap
to spring open
nest me inside
the other dolls
my wooden sisters
self-painted smiles
and braids
field of poppies
on black wool
it has snowed
first of the season
awakening me
I cannot leave
without embracing you
today is Eid
end of the holy month
where I wander without you.
see me as I am
open
behold me
as wounded as you
who knows how far
the heart can travel

through history
through flesh
through death.
I resign myself
to this love
lay the wooden doll
at your feet
open me
for I am yours.

Ramadan Postcard

for ME

The year your sister wasn't fasting
and your parents moved to the
Midwest – we sat in the kitchen
among the articles left behind
for division between the remaining
daughters and you made coffee
for me and your sister – dug
out holiday nuts and chocolate
we clustered around the table
the two of you with your hair down
your daughter joining us to table
with ladies this her first fast
no one making it a requirement
for faith. There is no formula
for the beneficial – no prescription
to reach the memory of light
when it redeems – no path
for divine reception in truth
the god moment lies on the table
the coffee discovered in the
cabinet the bitter chocolate
reminder that we make
our own joy your daughter
nine then with long hair and gold
earrings sitting between us – the boys
wrecking proverbial havoc in
the sun room – jumping
from couch to chair in their game
childhood is a noisy venture

a deliberate point of love – when I left
you covered your hair and
stepped into an abaya your mother
left in yellow, gold, and black,
the scarf billowing back
the youngest boy followed
us the miracle child born at twenty weeks
he graced the odds I was
surprised when he called my name – waving
goodbye – goodbye - goodbye as you both
disappeared in the rear view
mirror – a holiday
card tableau – and end of summer postcard
a Ramadan blessing
for the stranger.

Abaya: a full-length outer garment worn by some Muslim women.

Remains

In the light
the night tired
edges spent
dog eared like a book
we have read and given
over to the tight
remains of a gaudy night
soft after we return
turned back
turned inward
flame burning
unstoppable and bright.

FIVE

Texas Love Poem #2

Big is your heart
and grave to your making
I will set myself to your love
a thunder to the landscape
rain and flood and wild horses
in your father's corral
I am standing opposite your desire
slender and humid to be opened
kissed and made more than content
you are the very heart of Texas
never subdued but all ways
singing your self- soul to the tempo
soul of the story
soul of the earth
soul to my soul
heart of weeds and roses
play and sing
and dance me to the end.

DESIRE
(TEXAS LOVE POEM #3)

There's a flood in southeast
Texas and you tell me
it's been raining for two
days in Lubbock – three people
dead - the earth
drenched – I'll look beyond
and count the days
before you
arrive – it's now one
spin short of a full month
I'll count the miles as you fly first
to Houston and then east to me
I'll count each star that burns
the darkness into milk
each bird that moves
across the turning golden
trees outside my window
I've counted years from
my making – my child's birthday
in a row of candles
I've counted only on myself
to make life happen
to watch each cycle turn
with blood and light
but now I'll count with you
to make that moon shine splendid
against a boundless night.

A PHOENIX NEST OF VALENTINES
(TEXAS LOVE POEM #4)

The October light
sunrise early in the east
the black smoke sky on Venus
fire – orange and gold
the shiny crows gather
to the slender trees
a hawk circles
high and awake
I watch from inside
the cold morning calling me
out of my dreams.
I miss you already
before arrival
the sun hasn't risen yet
on you – the stars still give
Texas their light – when you hold
me in your hands imprint
their map onto my flesh
take up my open heart
in a phoenix nest
of new valentines
press me close
let your blood come hard
satisfy me into the future
brand me, the thunder of your heart
ignite me
and I will burn and burn
and burn
the luminous morning
out of night.

The Needle – the Thread

What am I supposed
To do with all this sorrow

Thread the needle, leave the table
filled with leftover Easter – chocolate foil rabbits

Marshmallow bunnies – sweet things I
Have to gather up and stuff into gris gris bags

To stun your diabetes into shame
We'll take them out at midnight

One at a time – strip them of their golden foil
Break off their long sweet

Ears and take in tiny bites between
Coffee in your grandmother's sepia rose

Cups – way too delicate for a family
Of cowboys and the lariat turned to lancet

We'll read your numbers in the dark
And when you are not looking

I will thread the needle – leave the table
Wiped clean – sugar bare with coffee

Cups and crumpled foil – what am I
Supposed to do with all this sorrow.

THE MASK

In love
I become you
resemble you
our bodies twist
turn the careful push
of sex, it is
your heart I want
to enter me, crack through
my ribs, push painful
pierce to my side, left
lanced I want your heart
to encircle my own
reason for memory
I want to kiss
until there is no air
no space, joined together
heart and loins.

I want to wear your face
know your joy, eat your fear
so I will understand
what it means to be a man.

Two Girls Ago

after Lucie Brock-Brodio

No hiding journals under the mattress
No whispering on the white rotary phone
No walking to school in the grey quiet

No sharing of poems in the hallway
No pretense of misunderstanding
No fear that the world ended on your street

No waiting for you on the corner
No need to accept what could never happen
No desire to be heartbroken, again

No symbolic gestures in absentia
No convoluted haunting conversations
No forgiveness in the face of betrayal

No side glances in the high school hallways
No watching the girls who came after
No need to forge my laughter

No memory to hold onto forever
No cards, no photos, no gifts
No trace of our love lasts on paper.
And this is reason enough to let live.

ONE MORE LINE THAN A SONNET

I found you last night on the web
no longer the handsome boy from upstate
New York native to the town where they hold the state
Fair, we spoke Russian together when we
were 18 and lost the chance to have a family
at 20 and then again when I was 22 and you
couldn't care less or more your state
of negation and mine of despair; I enjoined pain
then – it was what I grew – where my talent
lay. Now – three decades later – you have
emerged scientist, businessman, developer
of a plastic used by soldiers – there was a photograph
of you bending this miracle fabric in your left hand
towards the camera, your once handsome face distorted.
For all my heart had held, I would not have known you anywhere.

LIFE PRESERVER

I threw you a life preserver –
something round – white and red
into the redolent sea of faces
on grey sidewalks and trees
that grew in Brooklyn – cracking
the dry pavement into humps
and ground unworthy of
roller skating or bike riding above
our walking carefully between
the neighborhoods where the mimosa
tree in your mother's yard yielded
perfume and soft pink memory – I reeled
you in but the Navy took you away
as I faded – a point in the concrete horizon
a girl with dark hair – the first love
you had let go when the sea became
Dark - Beware
a storm settles between us – the table
set for three – I always sat under the blessed
Mother – in her orthodox red and gold
the ottoman curve in the architecture
of the frame around her – the other
I sat behind the table where I made
mistakes and knocked over glasses
that spilled or the other two yelled
in concert – mother wiping up the
sour cream – not worth crying over
the father shaking his head – and I
wanted to be outside where the trees
grew in Brooklyn – even on our dead end

street – a block from the subway – where
I knew for a small token of no one's affection
you could make a choice – take the direction
either to the sea or into vast stone city.

INFINITE FOREVER

for Colleen

The honey locust trees fan golden
out to cast the early October memory
of forgetting when I turned the heat
back on last year – this is a wide season
of painful repetition – time does not
matter – it's only the light caught between
what is tangible and what cannot remain
your death is another hole in the pattern
another birthday that will pass and pass
unnoticed – just a twinge of no regrets
and finality – hereditary heartbreak
and ghosts – would you call out through
the long and lonely corridor – hear the sound
of your boots in the snow – the city lit
up at midnight – we'll catch a glimpse
of our former selves in the plate glass
downtown Christmas window – it's the
photo no one ever took of us together –
stretches out into the infinite forever
how do I say words in love language
that only the dead can hear?

The Deepest Part of Dark

for CR

My first love came
last night in the deepest
part of dark to welcome
me with open heart
and spoke of visits
yet to make, Capri
Sardinia and Calabria
the naval view
behind his tour of duty
now we talked
of time abridged
the decades
flipping fast from
where he first set sail
I stood lost
without redemption
with no amends
my first love came
once to whisper sad goodbye
his death called me
to put a hold on time.
We never came
back, tonight the visit
lost, no bitter photo
left to share, together
Capri, Sardinia, Calabria
we never made it there.

SIX

Putney Bridge Station

You are the ghost that keeps on coming
up the stairs from the tube –
walking ahead of me on Putney Bridge
your hair reaches the edge of your collar
and I know that you have nowhere to go
destination unknown – the grass in the brick
overgrown – each footprint as quick as air
evaporating in front of me – a torrid column
smoke stack – burnt paper – another way
to always say *goodbye*.

Salt Memory

Winter salt
consummate ice
February melt
memory dull
sublunary love
my childhood
home the snow
settles into our
bones, our homes
our hearts divided
by decades, as I reach
out your silence pushes
back an eternity
of haste – you cannot
escape the cold
snow in Georgia
ice in the Carolinas – sunny
Florida heat rising
where you could
retire early – 9/11
the ash shifting smell
of the dead
the far away
tremble for a
lost adventure
I came home
you know I came
home to check
on my parents
I came home to
see the city smolder

across the river
in Brooklyn found
your fire
station at dusk
reading the names
of the lost – you were
not among them.
First Love
the boy who cheated
suicide twice the sailor
the fireman
you never knew how
I came
to know
that you were still alive.

BANISHMENT

after Garcia Lorca

I've thrown sand in the eyes of my horse
and still he finds his way back
to your door.

I've witnessed the crucifixion
of your interrupted heart
rend itself backwards
until your semen reached
me and I tasted myself
from your mouth.

I've tried to ride
far away
but *far* is only the future
and *away* simply a banishment
my horse still gallops
back to your door.

I've settled for silence
of the swiftest kind
all the lines to my heart
severed
the lines on my hands
dropped the reins of my horse
and watched
you walk
heavy and angry and hateful
into your next war.

DERELICT SLEEP

Decades flow
backwards and the dream
presents you as a confident
man at 35 – you didn't age for
years – I hid you from sight
from air – out of reach
your messages read
and saved when they should have
been destroyed. I suffered
for this love – suffered without
reason – remembered the day
when my heart stopped – then
I put you away – another broken
marker in derelict sleep.

DISTANCE TO REMEMBER

How do I remember you? Without
the tell-tale machinations of being young
and insecure, a quarter century of silence
and the distance of some 3000 miles
beyond forgetting that separated us? No ruse of friendship
on my part to connect the dots between no use
to say a word, we had, *goodbye* twice that I
recall and many tries at keeping well enough away.

I have forgiven you but for the memory written on my body
knows what is brought up by returning to the scene of any
crime. Sincere, you told me you were sorry, but I only recall
the robin's egg blue of the bed sheets and tossed pillows. I was
young and hurt vulnerable to you, and wondered who had
slept there the night before I stood on the threshold
and you apologized for sending me the check with no letter -
the clinic fee we split after my insurance came through – I know
how cold and ugly you can be – I know the depth of my anger
and remorse. Now equal, this middle age we have both reached
separately, this is the way of the world, you thank me for writing,
but really, I'm only looking in from far away.

PORTIA

after Shakespeare

You see me Lord Bassanio, where I stand
Such as I am. Though for myself alone
I would not be ambitious in my wish
To wish myself much better, yet for you
I would be trebled twenty times myself
A thousand times more fair
But the sum of me
Is sum of something, which to term, in gross,
Is an unlessoned girl, unschooled, unpracticed
Happy in this, she is not yet so old
But she may learn; happier than this

I am such as I stand
and should you want to take me
thus, weighing in the complexties
the ambitions, the sum of me
is the fair sum of motherhood,
of marriage, of vows
of promises I keep
you see me as I am
where I stand, for myself alone
though now for you, to wish myself
much younger, trebled twenty times
more dangerous, more fair

Happiest of all is that my gentle spirit
Commits itself to yours to be directed
I am my soul, which is a thousand fair
and burning lights when you walk into the room

where I stand, such as I am
can you not see me,
the full sum of my love
an unlessoned girl, unschooled, unpracticed
with you.

TOM O'BEDLAM IN THE GARDEN OF EDEN

I get pulled back so easily
your voice, your eyes, your need
and I reappear, open and happy
to the next day that suffers me to stifle
the sorrow -- the beautiful early
autumn weather --perfect
I am in it alone - the silent
house where you never see me - don't ask
I won't tell but open myself
to your body frightened and charmed to an Eden you
were taught, but don't believe last night we
watched the Tigris and Euphrates flow, vulnerable
I will myself not to deception but mercy to forgiveness
and your love which unsettles me like the weather
a tempest fit for Tom O'Bedlam himself - naked and
disguised - leading the blind and the crowned
into the light.

JADE CICADA

Jade in the emperor's death
mouth – to the grave – all openings
closed – no breath – no air – no life
to enter to leave – the end should
be silent – you stop my mouth
with yours – tongue, teeth, lips
and I call from within, rising
to your touch – and falling
beneath your weight to balance
sense and desire, to measure
life and place myself – a jade
cicada – last of the accoutrements
for the mouth of the Han
Emperor – where his blood stained
the carvings – the last parts of his
life – where he was human and
not god - place yourself in me
my blood comes for you.

Peregrine

Promethean
in sight in sound in thought in
deed – where you go, I follow
a paper trail now two decades long
I saved all your letters, the poems
written for the counties of the land
of 10,000 lakes, where I have never yet
been, what resplendent sorrow did we
arrive at what destination unticketed
unheard of did I not read you correctly
but only read what you could show, what
a play that was all comedy ending with
two weddings and now separation the ring
that binds loosens, I am drained of myself
held steadfast to the earth, tethered like some
great bird of prey, lessoned, kept on a lead
line, and now in flight, I fall, I falter, I keel
the appetite and nothing comes my way.

DIDO

My hope
is equal
to fear
my dead
self, angry as the winter
months an ice queen
in a Russian fairy story
and you the
Eastern prince broken
beyond repair I am
no Dido of Carthage
to lay myself in fire and there
concoct a death most fitting
for lost love
and respect too
the semblance of the world
in a small piece of Africa. no this
is a winter's tale in the favored
cold combination of treachery
and desire.
I know this
piece of poetry and dance, I know
what sleep feels like and dreams too
I know tomorrow the sun will
rise and so might I willing
to defend my heart again
against you --against fate
against time -- in silence
the agony of knowing
you will not hold me up
and give me life.

OZ

From across the window
the wind rises
dust, birds, debris
cyclone forward
away as shadow
from me to you
this separation
mutes my heart
noting nothing
I can say any longer
moves body or soul
to the sun bright
brilliant winter
the way I love
the earth – hopeful
and sleeping ice
under my boots
ice in my eyes
ice a cross
my mouth
a cross
the room
in blue
your dark eyes
dart like arrows
my desire akin to
grief now
familiar - a pattern
in a scarf or table
cloth a decoration
for the home.

Spinning

You like it on top
of the world
of the universe
of your own game its
own failure postulated
abruptly – finding fault when
the wheel turns and takes
you down a notch – but you remain
the most intelligent
the most well-read
the most lyrical experimental
oh yes, best in show
the blue-ribbon winner
calculated by the companies
you keep – and when too close
for comfort comes – the bottom
falls out and you bare your teeth
werewolf toxins in your bite
always prominent – always tight
collecting dead relatives
and husbands by the score
and bottomed out you hit
the floor – face first
heart last – well read
well fed – the epitome
of female dread.

TEMPEST

The weather rules me
out of favor you recede
into the background unimaginable
that we were intimate in love
lost between ourselves and the world
spinning revolving we asked one another
to stay away – each day a test – harder
than those you gave me to prove love
or that I was different from the others
preceding and impeding us.
I hate this separation – the cold dark
spring – which returns with a vengeance
bringing my sorrow along for the ride
and everything I touch brings you back
there's nothing for me to do, but live it.

SEVEN

MY FATHER'S HANDS

Played with fire
Played with irons
Played with shoes
That horses wore
Proudly on hard packed
Dirt roads that led to the Border.

My father's hands
Played with girls
Played with guns
Went to war

My father's tethered hands
Dug the airstrip trenches
Survived the Russian
Winter marches
And sleeping in the
Silent Soviet snow

My father's hands
Survived the famine
In the East
Survived the madman
Hiding in the Kremlin

My father's hands,
Held the rail of the boat
That crossed the Caspian Sea
Fed the orphaned bear
And Learned to drive
Amidst the oil fields in Kirkuk

Where the prophet Daniel
lies my father's hands

Touched the Wall
The stones
The Sepulcher
The pyramids
The valley of the tombs
Of kings
The graves of orphans
And things friends left
Behind my father's
Hand held my mother's
Wedding ring and long black hair
Held my new born self
And breathed me pure into the winter air.

Lantern Festival

this stone
forest
Eden
of the dead
the little boats
of light
and paper
our fathers

forest character
and Cyrillic prince

we let them go
one little light
among many lamps
they struggle back
to shore
to us
we nudge
them forward
ourselves
together on
the live earth
the flowers brilliant
against the darkening sky.

REMEMBRANCE DAY

Once more the day of remembrance draws near.
I see, I hear, I feel you:
        Anna Akhmatova
        from Requiem

The first day of Pisces
nearly spring
water out of ice
the sun will rise
the birds search for food.

We say
kind words to make up
the indeterminable loss
again and again
something as benign as
He is always with you.
or
I knew him because I knew you.

No, He is only there
when you evoke him
when the heart and soul
find grief
as they do love,
And the body
bears the weight of loss
like Christ his cross.

The world,
it is the same
as it has been
for twelve months.
and the city
you grew up in
reminds you
that someone is missing.

I am three months along
myself from remembrance
I stand before you
my tears
and trembling mouth
to your silence
I kiss your immovable face
with heart and soul
encased in my slender
anatomy
I acknowledge
this terrible year that has passed
and the great loss
of your father.

BENIGN PROTECTION

for Paula

In the late spring – June – before summer
descends – haze and mirage my father's
death left a hole in the pattern, deep
and unfathomable I reached forward
to make meaning and we met at your office
in Columbus Circle the green park beckoning
tourists, natives, and thieves we walked
to the restaurant -- close by – whose name
I can't recall – a diner – on 57th Street in the cool
dark booth the red leather banquettes
menus sized like the *Times* I have always
wondered how they cooked so many dishes in
the hidden kitchen we have a glass
of wine – white and crisp – order food
that quickly comes and my missing father
enlightened by death wore the 20th Century
like a map I am tracing the route in our
conversation you lost your father at 14 – in the summer
before 10th grade – we four met once in the cold moon
starry winter on the corner
of Marlborough and Church
in front of the Temple Beth Emeth us, girls
in our maxi coats – yours forest green and belted
mine black, as every coat I ever bought – our fathers
standing in benign protection – on the verge
in my reckoning the ghosts of childhood
remain, incredulous and strong, silent
and long-suffering, beautiful
and awful as memory herself.

Summer

for my father

I want to memorize this
our time together – what we did
without her there to tell me
You wouldn't want this life
you're not cut out for it – and me
the child holding the reins of an unruly horse
as you took off its shoe and examined its foot
before putting the new one in place
for riding far away – from the dirt I had pulled carrots
shaped like mandrakes – or had stolen sour apples
that fell beneath the huge tree where yellow and green
caterpillars hung like earrings in the twilight – or sugar
I'd taken from the box in the pantry when she wasn't looking.
It was a fortune of smuggled goods
with which to win them over
to keep them still and nudging me for more
while you attended to their hooves.

She still tells me what to do
miraculously knows if I've lost something
she has given me – as I should only like
what she had – and I don't care – I take these
things – and wait for prescience to cover me
like a blanket – she misses you – and wants to die.
You are in every dream she has – they fill her up
to being young – and upon waking she reaches backwards
to you – left only with the bed half empty.

I'm dying to be honest
and sit her down to listen finally to me
to see me as I truly am – it's almost hopeless
and I cannot bear her cursing in three languages
for all the good it does her – it sends me into silence.
I've chartered the stars to find the constellation
of forgiveness – its open milky light inviting me forward
to resurrection – to love – to the familiar made over
against the odds of time and space.
I've memorized this, now, the young girl, her long hair
slipping from the braids – the mandrake carrot in her open
hand, the unruly horse tamed and looking at her
with trusting eyes and her blacksmith father
whispering in Russian,
Hold him – hold him tight.

OCTOBER REQUIEM

for Anna Politkovskaya

A thousand souls
to see you
and carnations
their powdery scent
to fill the ugly space
and candles to light
the darkness – it is a congregation
of the astonished
those who knew you
and those who knew
your words.
Brave is hardly enough
to describe your actions.
You who have eaten the knowledge
of your death foretold.
You who have negotiated with gunmen
listened where no one else
dared to even speak
You who have written
what should not have been
acknowledged. You who have taken
the plight of the ordinary
conscript against his commanding
officer – You who have said *they are human*
too in Chechnya. And after all that
you loved your county
and its broken people

in the face of skewed
democracy. Anna, I live
in the land of the free
and the home of the brave
but we don't see the flag-
draped coffins arrive – we don't
see the mother, the wife, the lover,
the father, the brother, the son, the daughter
waiting to take that body home,
denied our national grief – it's blood
for oil –God where he hardly belongs
divide and conquer – be still –
No one should die in vain.

When he came into the apartment
did you know
what did you feel
at that last moment
did you look at him
the hired assassin
and ask – *have you come to shoot me?*
or to fuck me?
It is the same
word in Russian
Did you beg for mercy?
Did you call out to the Mother of God?
Or did you stand there
and whisper
I have long been expecting you.

I won't cover the mirrors
40 days you'll wander the earth
come settle here – as you should

never die – be spirit to us all
instill your fearless heart among us
who take for granted what is
our birthright
the simple thing
the freedom
of our speech.

I HAVE BEEN TO SAMARQAND

for my father

Two years ago
May now as you made yourself
ready for death I wanted to
remain, relieve her of her duty
and be a good daughter.
You sent me home
to die with her
alone.

I have been to Samarqand
that final time
a journey by water
the dream geography more full
than life, the mosque, the church
the covered women singing
the Stations of the Cross
the goblin boat to take me back
by morning
I travel by train, north and walk
to the park, it's hot and burning
to see the icons at the Met
to look into the eyes of each
and every opalescent Virgin
in the house of the father
she guides the souls in comfort to Samarra.
Her eyes
follow me, at home

I present you a gift
war traveler
who prayed
at every house of the father
St. Sophia's in Kiev,
the Friday Mosque of Tashkent,
the Bucharian Synagogue on Sepyornaya Street
the tomb of the Prophet Daniel where his stolen
bones grow the stops along the bloody way
in Iran, Iraq, in Syria
then Lebanon, in Egypt
and Palestine,
in Bethlehem at the Church of the Nativity
where the Ottoman Turks
had made the doorways four feet high
to keep the wild horsemen out
to Jerusalem
where they meet God as three
a trinity of one almighty
city to destroy the houses of the father
a caravansary on the journey
backwards to Samarra
you put messages in the wall
went into the Holy Sepulcher
and stumbled along the Viva Dolorosa
saw the dome of the rock
where Mohammed rode
a winged stallion to Heaven
across the Mediterranean
in Monte Casino you protected
the mountain
then the monastery

and in Rome
lifted your face to the ceiling
of the Sistine Chapel.

Now hear
the word of God
as the pain goes through
you like hot lead
as your bones move
lengthwise into sleep upon the bed.
I have brought your last book
in prescience and redemption
in secret and in silence
open it, alone, look
study the compassionate
face of Mary
the distant face of Christ
the icons
we cannot escape
imprinted on us since
baptism, I hear you
pray and I pray too
for your life that spanned
the century
let the light hold fast
enter Hagia Sophia
the final house of the father
go then, backwards to Samarra
leave your shoes at the door
see Christ who never was
removed before your destiny
is achieved, explore.

Arise, and go
Vladimir
for the kingdom of Heaven
is upon you.

ACKNOWLEDGEMENTS

Heartfelt thanks to my husband, Terry, my daughter, Zofia, and a special thank you to R.D. Pohl for his summations, Gloria Mindock for her keen eye on the order of things and Jonathan Penton for his honesty and attention to many details.

"Fog" and "Peregrine" first appeared in *Shadows of the Future: An Otherstream Anthology* (Argotist Ebooks, 2013)

"What My Mother Remembers," "Mother Tender," and "The Darkest Days" first appeared in *The Buffalo Evening News*

"Virgin Birth" and "Divine Liturgy" first appeared in *Facets: A Literary Magazine*

"Easter Sunday 2017," "King's Chapel Burying Ground," "Green May," "The Deepest Part of Dark," and "Putney Bridge Station" first appeared in *Mockingheart Review*

"Bone Trinity" first appeared in *Quadrangle Magazine*

"Shakmati" first appeared in *@poetry2go*

"Misha na Severa" first appeared in *MadHat 15: Eye on the World*

"Tom O'Bedlam in the Garden of Eden" first appeared in *Pirene's Fountain: A Journal of Poetry*

"Jade Cicada" first appeared in *Unlikely Stories*

"OZ" first appeared in *Café Review*

"My Father's Hands" first appeared in *Muddy River Poetry Review*

"Lantern Festival" first appeared in *Earth's Daughters*

"Summer" first appared in *Fathers and What Must Be Said* (Rebel Poetry, Ireland, 2015)

The following poems appeared in Lubbock Electric (Argotist Ebooks, 2013):
Christmas
Twelfth Night
Texas Love Poem #2
Desire (Texas Love Poem #3)
A Phoenix Nest of Valentines (Texas Love Poem #4)
Banishment

The following poems appeared in *Benign Protection* (Červená Barva Press, 2016):
Mother Tender
St. John the Divine
The Three Kings
After Christmas
Snow Earth
Prayers for the Dead
Russian Orthodox Lent
Unnatural Acts
Ritual
Brighton Beach was Never Venice
Matryushka
Benign Protection
I Have Been to Samarqand

The following poems appeared in *Lubbock Electric* (Nixes Mate Books, 2018):
Mother Tender (2)
Autumn
Raccoon Night
Flight of Ghosts
Moon Milk
What Ends Up Meaning Nothing
Salt Memory

ABOUT THE AUTHOR

Anne Elezabeth Pluto is Professor of Literature and Theatre at Lesley University in Cambridge, MA where she is the artistic director and one of the founders of the Oxford Street Players, the university's Shakespeare troupe. She is an alumna of Shakespeare & Company, and has been a member of the Worcester Shakespeare Company since 2011. She was a member of the Boston small press scene in the late 1980s and is one of the founders and editors at *Nixes Mate Review*. Recent publications include *The Buffalo Evening News, Unlikely Stories: Episode IV, Mat Hat Lit, Pirene's Fountain, The Enchanting Verses Literary Review, Mockingheart Review, Yellow Chair Review, Levure Litteraire – numero 12, The Naugatuck River Review, Tuesday: An Art Project, Muddy River Review,* and *Mom Egg Review,* with forthcoming work in *Fulcrum*.

Other Titles by Anne Elezabeth Pluto

Lubbock Electric (Nixes Mate Books, 2018)

Benign Protection (Červená Barva Press, 2016)

Lubbock Electric (Argotist Ebooks, 2012)

The Frog Princess (White Pines Press, 1985)

Recent Titles from Unlikely Books

Swimming Home by Kayla Rodney

Manything by dan raphael

Citizen Relent by Jeff Weddle

The Mercy of Traffic by Wendy Taylor Carlisle

Cantos Poesia by David E. Matthews

Left Hand Dharma: New and Selected Poems by Belinda Subraman

Apocalyptics by C. Derick Varn

Pachuco Skull with Sombrero: Los Angeles, 1970 by Lawrence Welsh

Monolith by Anne McMillen (Second Edition)

When Red Blood Cells Leak by Anne McMillen (Second Edition)

My Hands Were Clean by Tom Bradley (Second Edition)

anonymous gun. by Kurtice Kucheman (Second Edition)

Soy solo palabras but wish to be a city by Leon De la Rósa, illustrated by Gui.ra.ga7 (Second Edition)

Blue Rooms, Black Holes, White Lights by Belinda Subraman (Second Edition)

Scorpions by Joel Chace

Ghazals 1-59 and Other Poems by Sheila E. Murphy and Michelle Greenblatt

brain : storm by Michelle Greenblatt (Second Edition, originally anabasis Press)

My Hands Were Clean by Tom Bradley (Second Edition)

Made in the USA
Columbia, SC
26 June 2020